Perfect
PR

The Perfect Series

ALL YOU NEED TO GET IT RIGHT FIRST TIME

OTHER TITLES IN THE SERIES:

The Perfect Appraisal by Howard Hudson

The Perfect Business Plan by Ron Johnson

Perfect Business Writing by Peter Bartram

The Perfect Career by Max Eggert

Perfect Communications by Andrew Leigh and Michael Maynard

The Perfect Conference by Iain Maitland

Perfect Customer Care by Ted Johns

The Perfect CV by Max Eggert

Perfect Decisions by Andrew Leigh

The Perfect Dismissal by John McManus

Perfect Financial Ratios by Terry Gasking

Perfect Freelancing by Sean Marriott and Paula Jacobs

The Perfect Interview by Max Eggert

Perfect Marketing by Louella Miles

The Perfect Meeting by David Sharman

The Perfect Negotiation by Gavin Kennedy

Perfect Presentation by Andrew Leigh and Michael Maynard

Perfect Recruitment by David Oates and Viv Shackleton

The Perfect Report by Peter Bartram

The Perfect Sale by Nick Thornely and Dan Lees

Perfect Stress Control by Carole McKenzie

Perfect Teamwork by Ron Johnson

Perfect Time Management by Ted Johns

Perfect PR

ALL YOU NEED
TO GET IT RIGHT
FIRST TIME

MARIE JENNINGS

ARROW
BUSINESS BOOKS

Published by Arrow Books in 1995

1 3 5 7 9 10 8 6 4 2

© Marie Jennings 1995

Marie Jennings has asserted her right under the Copyright, Designs and Patents Act, 1988, to be identified as the author of this work.

This book is sold subject to the condition that it shall not, by way of trade or otherwise, be lent, resold, hired out, or otherwise circulated without the publisher's prior consent in any form of binding or cover other than that in which it is published and without a similar condition including this condition being imposed on the subsequent purchaser.

First published by
Arrow Books Limited
20 Vauxhall Bridge Road, London SW1V 2SA

Random House Australia (Pty) Limited
20 Alfred Street, Milsons Point, Sydney
New South Wales 2061, Australia

Random House New Zealand Limited
18 Poland Road, Glenfield
Auckland 10, New Zealand

Random House South Africa (Pty) Limited
PO Box 337, Bergvlei, South Africa

Random House UK Limited Reg. No. 954009

Set in Bembo by
SX Composing Ltd, Rayleigh, Essex
Printed and bound in Great Britain by
Cox and Wyman Ltd, Reading, Berks

British Library Cataloguing in Publication Data
A catalogue record for this book is available from
the British Library

ISBN 0 09 950811 7

ACKNOWLEDGEMENTS

In writing this book I have been greatly aided by many. In particular I would like to acknowledge the help of Michael Keegan, Sarah Watson, Godfrey Jillings, Anne Dewe (my literary agent) and Colin Thompson, Director of The Public Relations Consultants Association. I would also like to thank my husband, Brian Locke, for his help and support through the whole process of writing this book.

ABOUT THE AUTHOR

Marie Jennings has a long record of innovation – in several areas. And she is a prolific author.

Records of innovation span three key areas over the years: those of public relations, money management education and consumer affairs.

In the public relations area she was responsible for much development of professional public relations consultancy as Director of the Public Relations Consultants Association. This was in an era when public relations consultancy was little understood. During her stewardship the fees of member consultancies grew from just over £7 million annually to over £100 million annually. In this period she wrote extensively and initiated many key projects to enable companies to recognize the potential benefit of using professional public relations to help achieve their corporate objectives. Her books on the subject include *Getting the Message Across* and one of the earliest books on the importance of business ethics, *The Guide to Good Corporate Citizenship* (both from Simon & Schuster for Director Books).

In the area of money management education she has been highly active for over 30 years. She has contributed regular financial columns to many women's magazines, including *Woman's Journal*, *Family Circle* and *Good Housekeeping*. Additionally she has innovated on national television, with the adult education series *Money Go Round* (LWT) and more recently with Channel 4's award winning series *Moneyspinner*. Her books on the subject include *Women and Money* (Penguin Books) and *Better Money Management* (Piatkus Books).

Marie Jennings is also well known in the world of consumer affairs. She is President of the National Association of Womens Clubs (a senior women's organization),

Chairman of the Money Management Council, (the UK's money education charity), and Chairman of the Legislation Committee of the National Federation of Consumer Groups (a leading grass roots consumer organization). In addition she is a Fellow of the Royal Society of Arts and is taking part in their important review 'Tomorrow's Company – The role of business in a changing world' as a member of the Network Co-ordinating Committee and the Ethics Working Party.

Marie Jennings believes implicitly in the importance of the individual. Her book *Ten Steps to the Top*, on how to achieve self development (Piatkus Books), provides a route map to this end. It is currently enjoying good sales in China!

CONTENTS

Introduction	ix
1. What is PR and why is it important?	1
2. The two key principles	7
3. The seven priorities of perfect PR	12
4. Getting the message across	19
5. Perfect PR – for an individual	28
6. Perfect PR – for a company	36
7. Perfect PR – for a product	45
8. Perfect PR – for a charity	50
9. Brushing up on your PR skills	56
10. Thumbnail case histories	60
11. Sources of help and information	66
PR jargon	68

INTRODUCTION

It may be that you have never thought of PR – or public relations – at all. It may be that you have. It is likely that you haven't given deep consideration to how your personal PR can affect, inhibit or help your level of success in life, your career, your personal opportunities, and even your happiness and quality of life. And you should.

That is what this book is all about.

Although it is a short book, I hope that you will find that it contains information of real value, whether you are a novice at PR, have years of experience of practising PR within a company, or have the responsibility for public relations activities, using the whole gamut of PR techniques and the services of outside specialist PR consultancies.

You neglect PR at your peril! Whether or not you consider that you have a specific PR role to fulfil, whether or not you desire to develop a PR role for yourself, the simple fact is that you need to know about PR. You need to know where you stand, in PR terms, right now. You need to know whether you are good or bad at PR, if you have skills which need to be developed, or to be learnt.

If you have responsibilities for PR you need to know which tools to use and how to set about meeting your particular objectives. Above all you need to know how to set about learning about PR, what it is, and why it is important to you. Then you can attack the challenge of becoming 'Perfect at PR'.

This book will, hopefully, hold your hand on this exciting, stimulating and important journey. It could make a big difference in helping you to get what you want out of your life. Use the guidance, tips and hints it contains to achieve your personal objectives. The thumbnail case histories, drawn from personal experience of a wide range of situations, should also help to identify challenges and options used to provide solutions and meet the objectives.

Above all, remember that to be (almost!) Perfect at PR is an achievable and desirable objective.

Marie Jennings

1
WHAT IS PR AND WHY IS IT IMPORTANT?

A lot of pomposity surrounds PR. It is a subject that today is written about endlessly. You can even get a degree in it – in the United States, and in Britain too. Let us try to cut through all the jargon and pap.

Putting it quite briefly, and simply, PR is about information, perception and communication. It is about sending messages and receiving messages. It is about those messages shaping opinion, creating motivation, getting results. And we all communicate – all the time.

That is where the simplicity stops. To be effective, PR has to be enormously sensitive, perceptive, simple and direct. It should be blindingly honest, ethical and hopefully transparent. Above all, it must appear to be effortless. But be warned. Many, many people have learnt to their cost that good PR isn't easy. The true professional makes it appear a doddle . . . but the integrity of the thinking, the sorting out of the message to be transmitted, the targeting of it, the timing – all this needs to be thought through before the final gloss is added to make it all appear as simple as falling off a log!

In other words the message transmitted must cause the receiver to accept it, to agree with it, to act upon it. And the receiver must be carefully selected, with a lot of background knowledge about his or her attitude, thinking, likely responses, etc.

PR 'influences' people. And Perfect PR makes a 'helluva' difference to what can be achieved, whether it is on a macro scale – in relation to international politics, industry, business – or on a micro scale – in relation to personal objectives.

SOME POPULAR MISCONCEPTIONS ABOUT PR

There are, of course, many popular misconceptions about PR. Some of the most often quoted are:

- 'They are the gin and tonic brigade – the "stomach men and women".'
- 'They try to persuade you that their clients make and sell gold bricks.'
- 'They trade in half truths and too often hide the truth.'
- 'They are the "square pegs in round holes", the hacks who can't get jobs in the media or are past their "sell-by" dates.'

To believe any of these statements would be to do an injustice to the many thousands of good professional PR men and women working in industry, business and the charities in this country. In today's business world public relations is a respected management tool, recognized in boardrooms up and down the country and abroad.

So how do the professionals define it?

DEFINITION OF PUBLIC RELATIONS

As defined by the Institute of Public Relations:

'Public Relations is the planned and sustained effort to establish and maintain goodwill and mutual understanding between an organization and its publics.'

Whilst from the United States comes this conceptual definition which is commended to readers:

'Public Relations is the management function that identifies, establishes and maintains mutually beneficial relationships between an organization and the various publics on whom its success or failure depends.'

THE PRIORITY OF ETHICS

At the heart of all good public relations practice must be the total commitment to good business ethics. This is a much more substantial factor in this profession, which trades in communication and persuasion, than in many other commercial, industry and business management spheres that use PR.

Today public relations is big business. Tomorrow it will be even bigger business, because the increasing rate of change and the onward march of technology will mean greater priority has to be given to the overall subject of communications to stimulate motivation and action.

THE IMPORTANCE OF KNOWING YOURSELF IN PR TERMS – THE CRITERIA FOR SUCCESS

It goes without saying that, to be good at PR, you should be someone who genuinely likes people. At the heart of a successful practitioner is the genuine belief that most things are achievable when there is a proper dialogue of 'equals' between the parties concerned.

But liking people, and getting on with them, is only a small part of the whole. There are other requirements which need to be assessed. These include:

Your qualities

Would you say that you have a good measure of sound common sense? Have you a good level of self-motivation? Are you enthusiastic? Basically, would you say you are a positive person? Are you curious, a good or bad listener? Have you got 'staying power' when things aren't going your way?

Your skills

Are you good at putting your thoughts on paper? Are you crisp, lucid, logical? Are you a good speaker? Are you persuasive, objective, clear – at meetings, with larger groups, in public?

Your knowledge

Are you good at finding out and marshalling the facts of your case? Can you identify the positives and the negatives? Can you analyse priorities? Have you got a good 'nose' for business, for management procedures, for financial priorities? How well do you know and understand the media and how it works? Do you understand marketing (the subtle differences between advertising and selling), and what attributes those in PR need to put across to those who might use their services?

Your abilities
Are you 'confident' in your abilities, in the correctness of the case you are presenting? Can you make and carry through decisions, even when the going gets rough? Can you analyse and solve problems? Above all, are you prepared to pick up and take responsibility?

HOW TO FIND OUT WHERE YOU STAND
To find out where you stand, score yourself 1-10 on the above points. And, perhaps even more important, get a good friend or business colleague to do the same for you (and you may like to offer to do the same for him or her).

- Your qualities score
- Your skills score
- Your knowledge score
- Your abilities score

As a benchmark, if you consider you have scored 30+ this is good, if 20+ this is reasonable. If, however you have only scored 10+, recognize that you have a problem!

Use this information to help you to plan ahead in terms of improving your skills in relation to public relations techniques.

YOUR POSITION TODAY IN PR TERMS
Here is a further checklist to help you to define your position today in PR terms.

WHAT IS PR AND WHY IS IT IMPORTANT?

- Are you self-conscious? Many people are. If you are a person aspiring to be 'perfect' at PR you will try to manage this trait (if it exists), in the knowledge that it could inhibit your development and effectiveness as a catalyst.
- Are you versatile? There is often a need to be competent in a variety of areas.
- Are you flexible – in your thinking, in your ability to see several solutions to the same problem? And, most importantly, in your ability to see the viewpoint of others, from colleagues at work, to media, to those who oppose you and your point of view? Can you understand that opposing viewpoints may be equally valid to those who hold them – and see why?
- Can you cope with stress? All PR activity involves levels of stress for the simple reason that progress is being sought, change is being promoted, developments are being explained. The person who aspires to being perfect at PR will welcome the 'adrenalin factor', and use it to advantage. On the other hand if you are someone who likes to avoid stress, it is critically important to recognize this fact as soon as possible. Then you can plan your activities accordingly.
- Finally, how ambitious are you? Good PR thrives on energy, drive, enthusiasm and ambition. Recognize whether or not you are a person always ready to walk through an open door, and not afraid to take a calculated risk. If not, it is as well to be aware of this fact.

FOOTNOTE
You are involved in PR right now – whether you recognize it or not. You have a PR 'image', impressions you have already given other people about you. You need to

know what this is, and whether or not you are comfortable with it. You also need to know how to improve it, and your understanding about the whole complex, exciting area of PR. It is very worthwhile.

2
THE TWO KEY PRINCIPLES

If it isn't visible it doesn't exist

Perception and reality can be different

Recognizing the importance of these two key principles can help you cut through a lot of irrelevant and/or unnecessary detail in PR and its administrative procedures. You must ensure that you always focus on the end result. And, in addition, you must remember that if your objective is not clear to you before you start then you might as well not start at all!

So let's take a look at these two principles and what they entail.

IF IT ISN'T VISIBLE IT DOESN'T EXIST

At the end of the day all successful PR activity has to result in action – by those who receive the message. This action may not need to be taken immediately. If it is a change of attitude which is being sought, the seeds have to be carefully sown; the 'green shoots' then have to be fed before the plant can mature and flower, to achieve its potential result. This all takes time, sometimes a lot of time. In the case of major changes of attitude involving large numbers of people, the time involved could easily be a generation. But the needs are the same in all cases: planning has to be done so that there is a visible result at the end of the day.

Measuring the effectiveness of PR is a subject which has defeated many academics over the years. That is not to say that there have been no achievements in this field. Some progress has been made. But the difficulties remain daunting. This is because the results of PR programmes can be so varied. At one end of the scale they could involve defusing an industrial dispute, or defeating a take-over bid; at the other end they could prepare for an entirely new product or service, or political philosophy. Yet again, the result could be winning a public opinion poll or referendum, or successful fund-raising for a charitable cause. In another, perhaps simpler area, the result could be the successful launch of a new product or technological development. On a personal basis the result could be the development of a fast-track career path, or the winning of a public appointment. The result could even relate to settling harmoniously certain neighbourhood, family or domestic problems.

Failure rates can be high, too. Very often a progidious amount of planning, co-ordinating and work on complex and expensive PR programmes can fail to deliver the results required. This is because the number of 'intermediaries' who handle the messages and interpret them can so often give a 'twist' which is unexpected, as a matter perhaps of timing, other parallel developments, or simply because insufficient planning has gone into determining the likely attitude of an intermediary such as a journalist or opinion former (perhaps even a Member of Parliament). This is where PR activity becomes absolutely fascinating, because the 'thinking-through' process calls for such large and high qualities of sensitivity and judgement. It can be much more convoluted than chess!

In addition to deciding the objective and the need for planning, much thought has to be given to the messages to be delivered, their targets, and the tools to be used in delivering them. These matters are dealt with in chapters 3 and 4 of this book. What is also important to understand at this point is that the 'tone of voice' of the messages – whether delivered in print or in discussion, privately or publicly, directly or indirectly (for example, through the media) – will differ from case to case. In designing Perfect PR you have to remember all the time that there will be instances where a whisper is more powerful than a shout. Indeed, there are many occasions when skilled influence may overcome power. Notable examples of this can be seen through the lobbying of carefully selected Members of Parliament in relation to briefing them in detail on complex issues of the day. As a result existing legislation is changed or proposed legislation is quashed.

PERCEPTION AND REALITY CAN BE DIFFERENT

Many years ago a distinguished Statesman addressed a large meeting on the subject of 'What are the facts?' He explained that, as a Cabinet Minister, his in-tray every day was full of urgent papers requiring decisions. But, as he came into his office, the very first things he had to deal with – before he could get around to his overflowing in-tray – were media comments made on television the night before, and in the press that morning. 'The *facts,*' he said, 'are not the real facts at all, *but what the people perceive the facts to be.*'

This is worth remembering all the time. You can see the evidence of it around you every day. Major issues of the day which concern us all may not be the issues we would like to be concerned with and/or recognize as vital, but the issues that have been selected by the media, promoted perhaps by single-issue pressure groups (such as Greenpeace), or particular sectors of industry, Westminster or Whitehall, and thrust in front of us, demand our time and attention. Thus there is sometimes an overwhelming instinct to look at a glass as half-empty, rather than to recognize that, in reality, that glass is half-full!

To bemoan this is useless. Sadly, it is a reality that issues are in the main judged by public perceptions of them and not by their realities. In the same way, it is important to recognize the important difference between emotion and logic. Both are critical in developing your case for Perfect PR, but when there is a conflict the emotional factor can be much more powerful than the logical factor.

So what should you do in determining your own position on these two vital issues?

HOW TO DETERMINE YOUR POSITION

- In all your planning in relation to a particular issue, programme or campaign, identify the desirable result. And then go further than that: identify acceptable fall-back positions. Above all, look failure starkly in the face, and identify what to you would constitute failure.
- In dealing with the areas of perception and reality, you will need to get a good, realistic concept of the current positions with regard to the perception and reality of the issue, programme or campaign in question. Then you should identify – perhaps, in the case of a commercial or other campaign (you may need to have the backstop of research on this) – what the gap may be between the current perception and reality, and the desirable changes which need to be made to either or both to bring them in line with your desirable result (which you have already identified).
- Then comes the hard work in thinking through how you plan, co-ordinate and implement, to make the necessary changes come about to bridge the gap.

FOOTNOTE

In terms of planning perfect PR, it is important to be very hard-nosed about the factual position. This is not easy. It is tempting, sometimes, to indulge in wishful thinking. But the good PR practitioner, and the person aiming to be perfect at PR, needs always to be mindful

THE TWO KEY PRINCIPLES

of the harsh realities, to recognize the gaps which exist between perception and reality, just how wide they are, just how difficult to close. And at all times you have to be very aware of the objective to be achieved, and the time-scale within which you have to work. Then, and then only, will you have a chance of ending up successful!

3
THE SEVEN PRIORITIES OF PERFECT PR

This chapter addresses the guts of the overall issue. This is to prepare a PR plan to deliver the required results. It should, of course, provide for adjustment along the way so as to keep the aims fully in mind, in order to achieve the objective.

So what are the essential elements in a PR plan?

THE PR PLAN
It is essential that this gives a specific picture of the objective, aims, needs, actions and target results for the specific situation, together with a schedule of activities and budget, and/or other resources to be deployed. Thus, the PR plan can act as a blueprint for action by all those who have a part to play in the process. In order to give you, the reader, a picture of what is involved, let us take a look at a fictional PR plan for a large international corporation, The Perfect Transnational Consortium (which, of course, is also fictional).

1. Setting the Objective
The first point to focus on is the objective for the PR operation. This should be written in brief, succinct language, and should express the result sought by the totality of the PR effort in the campaign involved. The component aims should also be written out concisely.

Here is an example:

THE PERFECT TRANSNATIONAL CONSORTIUM – PUBLIC RELATIONS OBJECTIVE

The objective of the public relations activity is to help

the Perfect Transnational Consortium achieve the understanding and support it needs to operate successfully in international markets. In pursuit of this objective, it is the public relations responsibility of each operating unit to set going the mechanisms required (i.e. to establish channels of communication with employees and other selected targets), and to use these effectively to generate favourable understanding of the operations, goals, policies and basic beliefs of The Perfect Transnational Consortium.

In addressing the objective, The Perfect Transnational Consortium has identified the following Seven Continuing Aims, each with its constituent goals:

i) *To develop a better, truer public view of TPTC – what we are, what we do, what we believe.*

- We are a worldwide enterprise whose products are doing important constructive work around the world.
- We have a strong commitment to service.
- We are a company which places heavy emphasis on research and development in our sector.
- We are a member of a successful and highly competitive industry which works together well in terms of its national and international contributions.
- We believe in high levels of integrity, ethics, achievement and quality.
- We have a sound, broad base of public support among our institutional and private shareholders.
- We are a well-managed enterprise.
- We are a good company to work for, with loyal employees we care about.
- We are a good company to do business with.
- We believe in transparency and keeping the public informed.

PERFECT PR

- We are a responsible corporate citizen.

ii) *To secure better understanding of the benefits of our operations and products where our manufacturing plants and service facilities are located.*
(Identify specific goals)

iii) *To establish better understanding of TPTC viewpoints on important legislative and governmental matters.*
(Identify specific goals)

iv) *To promote better understanding of the creative role of profit in contributing to a better life for employees and the public.*
(Identify specific goals)

v) *To contribute to an improved climate for business operations, and an improved community attitude on factors that make settlement and growth in a given country or location attractive to business.*
(Identify specific goals)

vi) *To build increased community confidence in and goodwill towards the company, its operations and its people.*
(Identify specific goals)

vii) *To inspire greater individual participation in public affairs.*
(Identify specific goals)

2. Identifying the desirable result and required motivation

It follows that with a 'wish list' such as the above, which of course relates to a major international conglomerate, there should be a detailed list which addresses each item in the objectives, and spells out in detail the desirable result and required motivation. For example, goals iii and iv will be calling for a special programme of liaison with opinion formers, government officials and the like. In turn, this will mean producing special materials to transmit the agreed messages.

In considering this matter overall it is important to recognize that there are different aspects of PR. These can be described as:

- Positive PR – Stressing all the positives of the situation;
- Negative PR – Deciding how to handle the negatives which may exist in a given situation;
- Aggressive PR – Going all-out to improve a certain situation.

Most public relations campaigns will contain elements of all three.

3. Deciding the target audience
Here again, the aims need to be interpreted in detail in terms of target audiences for each one, recognizing that at times these may be overlapping. What is essential, however, is to ensure that the messages transmitted are consistent, in synergy with each other and, above all, do not risk cancelling each other out. This can easily happen. For example, a company may wish to put a positive story about profit performance to its institutional investors, so that it can increase share price. At the same time, it may be planning to close a plant and have to explain a redundancy situation to its workforce at that plant. Such an issue needs sensitive handling for obvious reasons.

4. Refining the messages
The messages to be transmitted have been defined by the goal in the first aim. Each message will need to be further refined when the other elements of the plan have been put in place.

PERFECT PR

5. Planning how the message is to be delivered

This is where the whole spectrum of the PR tools comes into play. Some messages will be delivered during specific highlights in the company's year, for example the issue of the Annual Report. Others will need to have events built around them: they may need to be supported by special items of print, by special publicity material, through the inauguration of a sponsorship programme, through the operation of a special lobbying campaign of opinion formers, etc. Timing, always an important consideration, will be critical in this context, also budgetary considerations.

6. Planning and implementing the campaign

Ideally all public relations and/or public affairs operations should be 'owned' at the top of the company. There should be commitment from the Chairman and the Board of Directors which recognizes the integral nature of public relations to help deliver the Board's overall objectives for the company. Having said that, the operation will need to have a director to focus the activity, drive the campaign and be held accountable for its success or failure. This will be, in the case of a major organization such as TPTC, either a Board Director or a Director of Public Relations, or Public Affairs or Communications – as yet several names are in use for what is basically the same function. This person will be heading his or her own specialist staff and may very well call on the services of one or more outside public relations consultancies to help deliver certain aspects of the overall campaign. Today public relations consultancies come in many shapes and sizes, and they specialize in different types of activity, although some of the largest offer a public relations 'supermarket' facility, with capabilities across the range of the needs of potential clients. Most responsible public relations consultancies are members of the Public Relations Consultants Association (PRCA), which is the trade association for the companies. Their details are given on page 67 of this book. The PRCA offers a useful service to match member consultancies to companies with particular and specific needs for public relations activities. This is widely used by sophisticated and knowledgeable organizations as well as those who are just dipping their toes into the waters of using outside professional public relations experts.

7. Measuring the results

One of the most commonly used techniques in relation to assessment of PR success is for the company to establish a benchmark for measuring results, using research, before the operation of the PR plan. And then, at stages during the operation and on its conclusion, it is necessary to undertake further and similar research to track progress made. Many tools are used for this purpose, for example the established research companies or the newly emerging specialist PR evaluation companies, and also the companies themselves. These include interviews with special, identified, focus groups, to determine 'before and after' information levels and/or attitude changes. The process need not be a bureaucratic post-mortem.

In most cases, where a large organization is involved, there will be a careful check of the materials to be used in the project before the campaign. This can be critical to the success of the campaign, and there have been many cases where the specific tools to be used, in terms of print and/or other materials, have been extensively modified and even abandoned as a result of such checks.

The evaluation process should start with setting down the specific quantified aims and goals for each of the target publics, specifying a measurement strategy in each case. The plan should spell out those to be measured and why. In essence the whole process should be a rigorous audit of the finished project, warts and all.

VALUE FOR MONEY

In the final analysis, what has been done has to be checked against budget and other resources invested in the programme, and a decision will need to be made as to whether or not value for money has been achieved.

During the overall process the matter of accountability and ethical behaviour of the company must be kept well to the fore – ensuring that the claims made in the objective and the aims and goals are consistent with the behaviour of the company as a good corporate citizen. Essentially, early warning systems should be in place to ensure that prompt corrective action can be taken if the plan is in danger of being blown off course.

FOOTNOTE

This summary of the critical process of coming to grips with the essential elements in a PR plan is necessarily brief. The reader charged with the responsibility of preparing such a plan, whether on a macro or a micro scale, should be prepared to indulge in comprehensive reading of case history material related to successful PR operations. Such material is readily available from the two key organizations dealing with public relations, the professional institute (the Institute of Public Relations), and the trade association (the Public Relations Consultants Association). (See 'Sources of Help' on page 66 for addresses and telephone numbers.) Additionally, there are annual award schemes operated by these and other bodies, including media, to identify successful PR case histories. It is essential for the reader to be able to draw on a good level of background knowledge – if not experience – in this area before he or she sets about the preparation of what has to be a successful and effective PR plan.

4
GETTING THE MESSAGE ACROSS

THE IMPORTANCE OF BEING A GOOD WORDSMITH

In one sense it is simple to understand – words are the principal tools of the public relations man and woman. But that, of course, is too simplistic by far. We all know the saying that the 'pen is mightier than the sword', but this can only be true if the words being used are being used correctly – to persuade, to inform and/or to motivate – and that they are directed at the correct targets.

Skill at being, or becoming, a good wordsmith – using the spoken as well as the written word, and by extension the visual and other images which those words evoke – lies at the heart of perfect PR.

So how do you set about recognizing whether or not you are a good wordsmith? Use this simple checklist to find out.

- Can you express yourself briefly, succinctly?
- Do you use jargon?
- Are you often asked to explain what you mean?
- Do you tend to use long words?

If the answer to the first question is 'yes', and the answers to the other three questions are 'no', then the chances are that you either are a good wordsmith, or have the potential to be one – and be honest with yourself.

THE MASS MEDIA – REACHING THE GENERAL PUBLIC

The general channel of publicity – by which we mean mass media: newspapers, periodicals, magazines, trade publications, radio, television, cable, books, etc – is the most effective route to reach the general public. But to be perfect at PR you will need to know how to handle publicity, the role of information, and how the various parts of the media work. You will also need to know the values of those responsible for media before you can be really effective in terms of publicity.

Above all, you will need to remember that, to be successful, publicity initiatives must be well founded, honest and immediately recognizable as credible.

It is equally essential to recognize that publicity must not be seen as the froth on the beer, it must represent good quality beer. It cannot be used for any length of time as a substitute for good works or desirable corrective action. Its objective is to make something known – or somebody known. By itself it cannot sell goods, win elections or raise funds for a charity. It must honestly reflect the ideas and background facts before it can create the impression required and so stimulate the motivation needed as a result of the message received through the publicity.

Above all, it is important to remember that the mass media constitute a nation's public information systems, in which public relations plays an important role.

Breaking down the mass media in a book of this length is not easy. Suffice to say, briefly, that it comprises:

National daily papers
Now a dwindling number, but very important. Each has its specialist journalists covering different sectors from news to features to sport, from science to personal finance to education. In this context it is also wise to remember that it is very likely that readers of the national papers will tend to read only those portions of the paper

which interest them greatly, and the typical reader will only be reading, say, one quarter of the whole paper! For the rest, only headlines are likely to have any effect at all.

National Sunday papers

Also a dwindling number, but representing a very influential sector. The Sunday paper is usually read in more depth than the daily paper (its circulation is much higher and readers have more time) and it tends to emphasize its feature material, taking issues and exploring them in more detail. As with the daily paper, its specialist 'departments' are staffed with experts in the different areas who tend to move their jobs between the Sunday and National daily paper sectors.

Weekly and Regional papers

As the name implies, these will tend to focus on their areas and they are today enjoying a resurgence in popularity. They will tend to emphasize news of local government, education, public affairs and personal news.

Magazines, Trade, Professional and Specialist press

These are periodicals which focus on 'niche' marketing, and they can be very important in PR terms. They also provide vehicles for personal publicity used with skill by the ambitious man or woman. The consumer magazines in Britain, with their large circulations, are particularly influential. *Good Housekeeping*, for example, has a circulation of just over half a million and a readership figure of more than two and half million readers per issue.

Talented journalists will tend to move to the National press after serving with a trade or specialist publication.

Wire services and news syndicates

These offer economic and effective outlets, providing you have information with high interest for the general public and/or news of substantial significance and importance. The wire services offer instant, worldwide access to all news media, and can be influential beyond calculation.

Television and Radio (broadcast media)

Television is the most powerful of all mass media, indeed it is the communications phenomenon of the century. It offers great scope as a medium for getting particular messages across, but it can also be a double-edged sword for those who don't understand it or use it without sufficient skill. It has to be said that industry has taken a long time to come to terms with television and, until relatively recently, attempts to co-operate with television were inept to say the least. Now, however, the public relations profession has made great efforts to understand the opportunities offered by television, and has tried to train and educate their clients in industry to make the correct use of the medium and to be realistic about their expectations with regard to what can be achieved.

With radio, the medium has a 'softer' image, and the opportunities it affords the public relations industry are well recognized and well used. It also offers many opportunities for the individual to get his or her message across, and this could be exploited more by the ambitious person with something to say for himself or herself.

You only have to look at the activities of the many single-interest activist groups to see many illustrations of enormous exploitation of the opportunities afforded by radio and television. It is a pity that worthwhile individuals, charities, and even industry itself, are not as alert as to what can be gained by a greater depth of understanding of these powerful media.

As with the press media, television and radio are departmentalized and run by specialists in the different sectors: from news to sport, from science to education, etc.

Cable television
Now being recognized as a communications medium in its own right, Cable TV will offer many opportunities for additional publicity channels, as indeed do the satellite systems, videotext, teletext and other examples of the newer technologies.

Public Relations Advertising
This relates more to corporate or 'image' advertising, where the general message being put across is that the company is a responsible and ethical organization and, therefore, the services and products on offer are worthwhile. This avenue must not be ignored in any review of mass media. Though expensive, it can represent a most effective means of reaching the general public. It is most used for institutional advertising, public service announcements, image creation, and 'advocacy', relating to positions taken with regard to specific issues.

THE PUBLICS TO WHOM THE MESSAGES ARE ADDRESSED

The external publics
To influence the constituent publics of a company or other organization through an open-system approach of communication and interaction is indeed a complex task. Each of the publics has special elements in its composition. You can, however, break these down into four main segments for the purposes of discussion in this book.

The customers. By definition a company has no chance of a future if it has no current or potential customers. Nor has a charity any chance of success if there are no supporters willing to give it donations. 'Customers' means differing things to different types of organization, but their importance is the same. They pay money in exchange for the goods or services they buy. They are a prime target group for communications, and they are researched endlessly. However, it is strange but true that, in this country, there are very few examples of the long-term dialogue of 'equals', with panels representing customers, which could contribute much to the future planning and success of a business, charity or other enterprise. However, that is changing, and perhaps we will be seeing more imaginative initiatives in this area before very long. Indeed, already there are some models which can be studied. BT, for example, is to be congratulated on its innovative record in this context.

In the meantime, we are all exposed weekly and even daily to incentive schemes of one sort or another to encourage us to become customers. We should, however, look forward to the day when, as customers, an organization considers us important enough to devote time and attention to letting us have a brief annual report, or to canvass our opinion about long-term issues that really matter (rather than the more usual case of asking what sort of nozzle we would like to see on the new shampoo bottle). And, hopefully, we will see more priority given to the 'engineering' of complaints systems in organizations, so that customers who complain are not considered second-class citizens but recognized for what they are. Direct, accurate, fast and sound research should be used to improve a product or a system, so that the company can plan for the future on a more secure base. It is a matter of research and record: one customer who complains and is handled sensitively may bring several new customers to buy the product concerned. Proper complaint handling can be very good business indeed! Things are improving in this context, but from a very slow start. And this is where the reader aiming at perfect PR can make an impact. In the 'Sources of Help' section of this book (page 66) you will find some addresses useful in this context.

The shareholders. Shareholders are today recognized as one of the key groups of stakeholders for a company, because they own the business and expect a return on their investment. Until very recently they were considered as first among equals. Shareholders are, of course, a most important group as regards company communications; also those who act on their behalf (for example fund managers). A lot of effort and money are today expended on the area called 'investor relations', which includes communicating with shareholders, etc. This is certainly a key area for the reader interested in perfect PR to study.

The community. The community represents the society within which we live. If a company is involved in its community it will be active in the areas in which it operates, as well as its direct markets, and also local public affairs and the like. Today community relations are, rightly, being given more emphasis by organizations large and small. This is right and proper, since areas covered include the environment, health, safety, education, local amenities and the like. Good relationships with its neighbours in the community, which may mean almost everyone, are crucial to an organization's success in the long term.

It is very important to remember at all times that the community is a miniature of the national public and the birthplace of national opinions.

The opinion formers and other specialist audiences. Opinion formers are many and various. They can vary issue by issue. In most cases they include the Members of Parliament of both Houses interested in the organization or the issue, the Whitehall officials with responsibility for dealing with them, the educationists interested or involved, the trade and professional organizations with responsibilities in the area, the relevant industry leaders, the interested lobbyists, the relevant specialist journalists in differing sectors of the media, and so on. In most sophisticated companies there are carefully crafted and regularly updated lists of opinion formers who are sent relevant material from time to time, and are briefed on the progress the organization is making or difficulties it is experiencing. The purpose is to get the understanding, help and co-operation of the opinion formers on the opportunity, problem or issue in question.

Today the whole area of corporate public relations has developed, in order to cater for the wide and developing marketplace of communication, with opinion formers of one sort or another, nationally and internationally.

The internal publics
The internal publics of a company include all those who work for or with the organization, from employees to part-time salesman and/or other intermediaries, including suppliers and distributors.

To reach these groups is a simpler and more precise operation because it can be more closely controlled.

It includes the use of the printed word, in terms of the house journal or staff or works newspaper, pamphlets, booklets, bulletins and letters, inserts and enclosures of one sort or another, printed papers, bulletin boards and posters. Also, of course, the spoken word is a major tool in this area; it is used to communicate with the internal publics of a company, at committee and union meetings, formal presentations, etc.

In addition, when reviewing the internal publics of an organization, it is important not to forget that important and often vital tool of communication: the grapevine. Many are the cases where efficient use of the grapevine has aided management to get its message across,

GETTING THE MESSAGE ACROSS

and also vice versa – it is often used to alert management that all is not well amongst the employees!

OTHER TOOLS OF COMMUNICATION

These are many and various and can be used to address both internal and external publics. They can include exhibitions, displays, sponsorship of events, programmes or particular sports, and donations to worthwhile charities.

FOOTNOTE

It follows that getting the message across means weaving a complex web with varying communications tools and channels, directing messages at one or many more publics, internal and external. What is vital – and often not given the priority it deserves – is to ensure that the various messages being disseminated do not conflict with each other and cancel each other out! It is always wise to check this as your final communications operation.

5
PERFECT PR – FOR AN INDIVIDUAL

To be perfect at PR as an individual, you first have to know yourself thoroughly, warts and all. You have to look honestly at your strengths and weaknesses. The next step – if you want to work in PR, or need to apply PR skills in your own work – is to recognize the nature of the jobs in PR, and the ranges and types of skills you need to have, to learn or buy to apply PR techniques successfully.

Let us now take a look at these three separate areas.

Knowing yourself, in PR terms
This really means assessing what you have to offer.

Finding out about yourself is not easy. It was explained, many years ago, by a distinguished academic as recognizing that in actual fact you have three 'centres'. These are the 'head', the 'heart', and the 'hands'. Each human being has a need to engage each of these 'centres' to the right degree and in the right proportion to release the potential which that person is capable of achieving. But not all of us are aware of this, and if we are not sensitive to this aspect of our human needs we take a large risk of ending up frustrated, unhappy and even aggressive. Quite simply we believe that our worth isn't being recognized by others, but we haven't taken the precaution to 'know ourselves' sufficiently and plan our lives accordingly, so maximizing our potential.

So, your first need is to find out how you feel, and to decide for yourself what you want out of your life. This short checklist should help.

- Are you ambitious? Very?

- What aspirations do you have for yourself?
- Do you want to achieve wealth?
- Do you want to run a major organization?
- Do you want academic distinction?
- Do you want to achieve status, fame and/or become one of the 'great and the good'?
- Do you want to be at ease with yourself, with a happy and contented family life, and put this first?
- Do you react to challenge? Want it? Need it?
- Do you like to 'make things happen', welcome change, find it stimulating?

There may be others, more personal to yourself.

Your 'SWOT' test
Having gone through the above exercise it is now time to examine the key components of your strengths and weaknesses. Do this little 'SWOT' test on yourself:

Strengths – list these.
Weaknesses – list these – honestly!
Opportunities – list those which you can instantly recognize.
Threats – identify where you think these may lie.

Now, looking at your potential in terms of PR capability, you need also to examine certain aspects of your personality. For example:

- Are you gregarious?
- Do you find it easy to make conversation with someone you have just met?
- Do you make friends easily?
- Do people who meet you want to meet up again?
- Do you make the first move to keep in touch with others?
- Have you a sense of humour?
- Are you a leader or a follower?

PERFECT PR

- Can you work with (or for) people you dislike?
- Can you be interested in other people's concerns?

The answers to these questions will fill in some of the picture you need to have before you can establish what you have to offer in PR terms. In doing these exercises you may have found out one or two things about yourself which you didn't know before!

The importance of making a good impression
Presentation is an important component of success in PR. And personal presentation is key. The impression you make on a new acquaintance as you enter a room – the 'snapshot' you allow them to take of you – colours their opinion.

Most successful PR practitioners have carefully cultivated their appearance, grooming, voice and related matters to ensure that their personal presentation maximizes their value. And we have all read about the voice training, grooming and other advice given to national and international politicians to ensure that they, too, make a good impression. It is important for you, too, to ensure that you pay this matter the attention it deserves.

THE NATURE OF JOBS IN PR
Having read earlier chapters in this book, which outline the Seven Priorities of Perfect PR and identify the PR tools, you will recognize that any PR operation must first identify the objective, the needs involved, the target audiences for the message, as well as the means and timing for delivering the message. This is valid in all contexts: in personal development, or in working within the PR business, either for an organization or commissioning outside PR. Following this, the priority is to conceive the way ahead, examine the likely effectiveness, and finally determine a plan of action. Now it is possible to take a look at the nature of jobs in PR.

PERFECT PR – FOR AN INDIVIDUAL

What do PR people really *do*? This is an often asked question. For the purposes of this book the many and different types of work have been divided into ten separate categories.

However, before this matter can be considered, it is important to recognize that there are two separate and distinct wings of the PR profession.

These are:

- Those who work 'in house' – on the PR activities of a company, other type of organization, or charity, and employed by that organization.
- Those who work 'outside' – in public relations consultancies, offering specialist and general services to clients in the manufacturing industry, retailing, trade associations, or political, community and charitable organizations, etc.

The top ten things PR people 'do'

1. ***PR people plan.*** Endlessly they plan, determining the objective, the needs, the priorities, the desirable ends, the targets for the PR messages, the time frame – and of course the costs! With their focus on the importance of ethics, PR people have often taken the lead in the establishment of codes of conduct and even codes of ethics in many areas of national and international business and industry.

2. ***PR people manage.*** They need to be able to administer the overall PR programme to ensure that it runs on time, to budget, and see it ends up with a successful record of achievement. It is true to say that until relatively recently some PR people did not rank well as managers: they were good as professionals, at handling the PR aspects of the task, but they didn't give as much priority as they should to the management function

itself. All that is changing now. However, for the person keen to be perfect at PR, it is important to recognize the need to hone up management skills as much as to develop the operational PR skills.

3. ***PR people liaise with others.*** They liaise with journalists, technical experts, politicians, academics, opinion formers of one sort and another, also with employees of the organizations concerned, with charities, community leaders and so on. All PR liaison should be to some agreed and identified purpose which helps achieve their overall objectives in due course. PR people in many countries have been leading the development of 'networking' – now widely recognized as a valuable communications tool – whereby people in complementary areas (and even in competitive ones) meet together to form a common cause on issues of importance.

4. ***PR people organize and administer.*** They arrange special events from press briefings and conferences, from annual general meetings and sales tours, to 'open houses' (the day when the company welcomes visitors to see the factory or offices) and anniversary celebrations, award functions and charity or sports sponsorship events.

5. ***PR people write.*** They write news releases, newsletters, letters of all sorts, to groups from opinion formers to journalists. They write reports, speeches, copy for booklets, posters, radio and television scripts. They write – sometimes as 'ghosts' for clients – trade paper articles, magazine articles, letters to *The Times*, etc. They prepare proposals, technical materials and the like.

6. ***PR people edit.*** They edit house journals, newsletters, reports to shareholders, letters written by their peers on occasion, other communications prepared by

technical and other experts for dissemination to external and internal publics.

7. **PR people produce.** They have the responsibility for welding together many aspects of communication involving the use of print, photography, design, art, audio and video materials, so that these are created into the communications tools which are needed to transmit the messages relevant to the job.

8. **PR people speak.** They speak at meetings, at presentations, at press conferences, in front of television cameras, on radio shows, at private and public functions of one sort or another.

9. **PR people research.** One of the main areas of activity for PR practitioners is the gathering of intelligence, and they have to be good at it! They need to know where to go for information, what to look for, how to analyse it and monitor and update the information, evaluating it so that it can be 'mined' if needed to assist the campaign or project on hand.

10. **PR people train.** In this still relatively new profession it is ever more important to ensure that there are training opportunities available for the bright young sparks who will be leading the business tomorrow. In the main it is true to say that PR people are generous with their time, knowledge and experience to help young people understand the challenges and opportunities in following a PR path.

Naturally enough, not all PR people are good at everything! And, it has to be said, on occasion there is an overwhelming need for PR people to be tough – tough at withstanding jetlag, able to walk off a plane after many hours in the air, and into a tricky meeting. And, also, there are occasions when they need to have tough livers!

Altogether a daunting picture to look at – to be perfect at PR . . . but nevertheless exciting, stimulating and even rewarding in the last analysis.

APPLYING PR SKILLS TO YOUR OWN CAREER (AND/OR LIFESTYLE) DEVELOPMENT

Reading through the above text, and undertaking the little exercises involved, should go a long way to identifying for you just which PR skills you need to apply to develop your career (and/or your life) along the lines you would like. If you add to the above the need to be 'visible', and the important differences between 'perceptions' and 'reality' covered in Chapter 2 of this book, you should be clear as to the moves you need to make to climb your own ladder of success.

EVALUATING RESULTS

Having started on this road, it is most important for you to stop, from time to time, and look at what has been achieved. You will need to leave a good period of time (for progress to be made) before you can really assess what has been achieved. However, a good discipline is to give yourself a six-monthly cycle to examine whether or not you have made progress towards your objective – whether it be personal or corporate. Prepare a very short checklist which is appropriate to you. State the objective you want to work towards, the measures you are trying to take, and then simply record on a scale of 1-10 the progress you have made. You may be in for a pleasant surprise!

FOOTNOTE

In reviewing this area overall keep the following two basic facts well in mind:

- People in general fall into two categories: those who want to *be*, and those who want to *do*. Recognize which category you are in.

- Most people who get 'to the top', whether it be in the business world, the academic or the art world (and others), get there because of the standards they have set themselves . . . not the standards others have set for them. Try to ensure that you set PR standards for yourself as you consider the points raised in this chapter.

6
PERFECT PR – FOR A COMPANY

For a company to have Perfect PR, certain facts should be recognized. For example, the fact that management itself is, essentially, based on an information system. Broadly speaking, management receives two kinds of information:

- Instructions from the Board or top management
- Information about the environment in which these instructions have to be interpreted. This will include the marketplace, the shareholders, and all other 'stakeholders' in the organization.

At the lower levels in the company, the instructions have to be clear and precise, and the task of interpreting them is easier. At the higher and executive levels the information is less complete and less precise, whilst at the top perhaps it doesn't exist at all, and those in charge have to create policy from the information they are able to imagine or themselves glean from the environment. The overall process is many faceted, and the company needs to exchange information with all its stakeholders in a continuous dialogue about an ever-changing scene. For a company, Perfect PR is an essential component to ensure success in all the company's dialogues.

The above view assumes a 'from the top down' management process. There is a move towards federal structures – so the pyramid has a much wider or flatter 'top' tier. In these cases, too, PR is an essential component to get the organization's messages across.

These stakeholders, to whom the company's corporate strategy has to be communicated, comprise the following groups:

The external publics

- Customers
- Customers' 'peer' and reference groups
- Shareholders and/or other controllers of capital
- Suppliers and service organizations used by the company
- Bankers, fund managers etc.
- Distributors
- Media – Press and broadcasting
- Consumer groups
- Community groups
- Environmental lobbies
- Relevant opinion formers, including Parliament, trade and professional bodies, etc.
- Also, of course, the organization's competitors

The internal publics

- The Board itself
- Middle management
- Shop floor
- Sales force
- Research and development staff
- Suppliers and service organizations used by the company
- Potential recruits to the company

All these stakeholders have information and communications needs which should be met by the enlightened company. They require different messages, delivered at different times, using different communications tools. However, it is essential that all messages are capable of fusing into each other and do not conflict and cancel each other out. The role of effective PR is essential to the success of management in handling all its communications.

How is this achieved?

In today's marketplace most companies have adopted either or both of two systems. They have prepared a 'Vision Statement', and/or a 'Mission Statement'. PR should be involved in both.

The Vision Statement
This sets out the way ahead as the company sees it. It declares where the management wants to place future development. It is philosophical, often 'blue skies' as well as 'green fields', and should include a major 'feel good' factor.

The Mission Statement
This sets out where the company stands here and now, where it wants to go, and how it wants to get there. It is the expression of agreed company policy, targets, principles and methods.

Overall, the company should be declaring its intention to be or become a 'Good Corporate Citizen', recognizing – as it was put some years ago by Sir John Harvey Jones – that 'No company exists in a vacuum. Each of us is dependent upon the goodwill and support of the members of the community in which we exist. It is only by constantly striving to maintain high ethical and environmental standards that we can renew this "licence to operate" on which our future depends.'

In both the above, the challenge for the PR practitioner is to stop either or both statements becoming too bland, meaningless and/or waffly!

THE PROCESS
Once a public relations problem or opportunity has been identified, using research and analysis, then ways of handling it must be defined. This involves planning and basic strategic decisions to be made before a plan of action can be written and agreed. It is essential that the

PERFECT PR – FOR A COMPANY

first two stages of the process are soundly processed for the third stage to be effective. Lack of strategic thinking and planning can lead to waste of money and failure, which can be enormously prejudicial to the company's record of achievement. If the company itself does not have access to the necessary experience and capabilities from within, it is important to recognize this and to choose the right type of public relations consultancy – offering the right mix of attitudes, experience, connections, skills and application – with which to work.

Having identified its mission, and the specific goals towards which it is working, the company should identify the objectives for its PR programme, preferably with advice from someone who knows how to set about this. Here is a snapshot of the process which should take place.

- Planning should ensure and determine what work must be done overall.
- Mission and roles should be defined – identifying the nature and scope of the work to be done.
- Key result areas should be identified. This should lead to identifying and setting out where resources of time, talent and money are needed.
- Key performance indicators should be identified to establish measurable factors on which the objectives can be set.
- Objectives should be set out and agreed, together with measures to determine the extent of their achievement.
- Action plans should be prepared and agreed – with achievable results set out. These should include:
    Programme of activity
    Schedule of timing
    Budgeting requirements and assignment of resources
    Reporting and accountability procedures

Any piloting or testing procedures
Review procedures.

WRITING THE PROGRAMME

There are many ways in which this process can be handled, and there are several sources of help and case histories to which the reader aspiring to be perfect at company PR may refer. Some sources of help are identified in Chapter 11 of this book.

Here is one suggested formula:

Objective

Give a short definition of the company objective – for example: 'To introduce effectively to the consumer a new method of distribution for speciality food products.'

The problem or opportunity

Give a brief summary of the problem or opportunity – for example: 'Problems identified include (a) Consumer resistance to change, (b) . . . ' etc.; 'Opportunities identified include (a) Access to fresher products, (b) Pricing advantage for the consumer, (c) More convenience, (d) . . . ' etc.

The plan

Set out brief lists of the action to be taken (to include meetings with specific groups, liaison processes, media relations, print to be prepared and circulated, etc.) – for example: '(a) Organization of Launch Programme for relevant media (trade, specialist, consumer), (b) Schedule of briefings for consumer organizations, opinion formers, community leaders, etc., (c) Release of background research, (d) Promotional tour, (e) Follow-up media campaign on success of launch, (f) . . . ' etc.

The communications programme

Set out in brief bullet points all the methods by which the company intends to communicate its position – for example:

PERFECT PR – FOR A COMPANY

- Press and broadcasting media information packs
- Schedule of press releases
- Background factsheets about research, endorsements, etc.
- Biographies with photographs of key personnel connected with the initiative, etc.

Timing
Schedule of timing to include planning and co-ordination phases, also production phases (to include authorization) for all items of print, information etc. to be used in the overall campaign.

Budget and Resources
This needs to be set out in detail, and authorizations and re-examination procedures are necessary to check costs are within budget at all times.

Evaluation
Identify agreed methods of evaluating results (by research, through people who have purchased a new product, by media comment, etc.)

EVALUATING RESULTS OF PERFECT PR FOR A COMPANY
This is the hardest part in the delivery of Perfect PR for a company. As stated in another section of this book, much work has been done in this area but, alas, much remains to be done. However, here is a formula which can be considered:

The first priority: Reputation

The reputation of the company is an essential component of its long-term success. This relates to its record of good corporate citizenship, and can provide some signposts by which the reputation can be measured. In the final analysis it *must* be commercially successful, now and in the future. Here are those top ten signposts.

The Good Corporate Citizen:

- has a mission statement, and a set of corporate beliefs and values which drive it;
- recognizes the need for the mission statement to be 'owned' by all members of the company;
- tells the truth. How else can a company live with itself, let alone with the other citizens who are its neighbours?
- is open with the community – tells them what it stands for;
- will communicate – a sufficient amount, and more than strictly necessary (it must never be too little!);
- is approachable by all;
- is generous of time and resources for relevant 'worthy causes';
- is visible, shows up;
- keeps in touch (with local schools, clubs, societies, etc.);
- initiates projects, helps to provide ideas, helps others who generate ideas, encourages, and helps as a catalyst.

Acting with enlightened self-interest, the Good Corporate Citizen recognizes that good continuing business needs good ethics.

THE ROLE OF THE PUBLIC RELATIONS CONSULTANCY

As has been said earlier, the use of a professional public relations consultancy should be considered whenever a company is planning a pro-active PR operation. If so, the method of selecting a suitable consultancy takes a high priority. How is this done? Here is a preliminary checklist:

PERFECT PR – FOR A COMPANY

- Decide in as much detail as possible what you want a public relations consultancy to achieve for your company, and what budget is available to this end.
- Select a number of consultancies to consider.
- Ask the consultancies for information about themselves, their clients, terms of business and relevant expertise. Ensure they have the experts and facilities you may need (for example international offices, specialists, test kitchens, etc.).
- Reduce your list to no more than six, and visit each personally to see the working environment and meet the staff who would work on your account.
- Draw up a shortlist of not more than three consultancies, and invite them to 'pitch' for your account. Brief them thoroughly so that they can draw up detailed plans of their approach for you to consider.
- Give the consultancies a realistic amount of time in which to prepare their presentations. If you want more than outline recommendations, ask how much this may cost.
- Ensure that all your relevant personnel (including final decision-makers) are present at the consultancy presentations.
- Trust the consultancies as much as you would trust other professional advisers, for example the company's accountants and lawyers.
- Appreciate that professional public relations is not a universal panacea for quick results. It is also opportunistic.
- Before signing a contract with your chosen consultancy, ensure that all parties are agreed on the work which will be done, how much it will cost and how you will work together, with relevant accounting and reporting procedures in place.

FOOTNOTE

Above all, the reader aiming to be perfect at company PR must remember that actions speak louder than words. Also, the company must be visible, and the perceptions of it should match the reality as closely as possible.

7
PERFECT PR – FOR A PRODUCT

The first point to remember when considering perfect PR for a product is that PR is not marketing. The differences between the two must be understood. Confusion between the two happens often, and should be recognized. Perhaps confusion happens most frequently in small organizations, when both public relations and marketing functions may have to be handled by the same person.

The confusion can also arise in non-profit-making organizations and charities, where 'non-profit' marketing or 'social' marketing is used to build and maintain relationships with members, donors and other non-consumer constituencies.

A couple of definitions of public relations are included on page 2 of this book. Let us now take a look at a definition of marketing.

A DEFINITION OF MARKETING
Marketing is the management function that identifies human needs and wants, provides products to satisfy those needs and wants, profitably, and results in transactions to offer and deliver those products to the potential user.

Marketing requires proper research to define the needs and wants, substantial analysis and research to establish the nature of the product to be designed to meet them: the design of the product itself, its packaging, the communication of its benefits, and its distribution. Marketing includes the use of advertising, sales promotion and public relations as some of its essential elements.

Basically, marketing shows your customers and potential customers where you stand in relation to your competitors, and identifies (hopefully) all the ways in which you are superior!

Product publicity and promotion are often used to help achieve marketing objectives. In this context public relations can be used in a support role to help the overall marketing effort, through the writing and placement of product publicity stories, the planning of events, and presentations to special groups, as well as the co-ordination of media support to achieve coverage of the new product and its benefits.

Clearly good public relations can help to ensure the success of marketing effort.

PLANNING AND SHAPING THE PR EFFORT

So, how does the person entrusted with the public relations support programme for the introduction of a new product set about planning and shaping the PR effort so that it is perfect?

First of all, the PR effort must be the subject of an agreed PR plan within the overall marketing strategy, which sets out the objectives, the target groups involved, the messages to be transmitted, the media involved, the timing, and the budget and other resources to be accessed.

The priority here is to identify and gather together all the information possible on the new product. This includes all relevant research – about the need for the new product, why it will fill a public or specialist gap in the market, its design and/or formulation, its packaging, etc. Clearly there will be a need to study the marketing plan. The PR practitioner will be looking to assimilate the facts to present a strong case for the product, also for

PERFECT PR – FOR A PRODUCT

items to add 'colour' to the basic story and make it more attractive to others. For example, there may be someone of significance related to the development of the product, something unusual which happened and which could be used to add this 'colour', some new 'twists' which could help add to the appeal of the story in the search for publicity. Health and safety aspects of the new product will need to be explored carefully.

- At all times the PR practitioner will be seeking to establish what is and what is not 'new' about the product, its packaging, and its distribution. He or she will remember that any 'claim' made about the product will need to be established and substantiated.

- Then the PR practitioner will look at the user groups interested or involved with the new product. It will be necessary to establish whether or not some aspects of these groups could be developed for publicity purposes. It may be that a prominent person can be used in connection with the product to 'endorse' its importance, ensuring that picture editors have a familiar face which readers can recognize to illustrate their stories about the introduction of the new product. (Buyers, editors and consumer purchasers all find it useful to have an already-known 'peg' on which to hang new information.)

- Now comes the matter of establishing the media most likely to cover the stories of the new product. These will range from trade, professional and specialist to national and international press, regional media and, of course, all the broadcast media (Radio, TV, Satellite, Cable, Internet, etc.). Schedules will be drawn up to conform to the printing dates, the advance 'lead' times necessary to plan the campaign so that maximum momentum can be achieved. In the case of a national monthly magazineusing colour, for example, the advance time will be to the order of 3-5 months. This needs to be taken into consideration at the planning stage, and will include the examination of whether or not exclusive stories can be placed, thereby accommodating the long advance timings with minimum risk of the story getting out too early, or being 'spiked' (not used) or delayed. Timing can be critical to success.

- Having established the media to be used, there is the critical matter of drawing up the storylines for the releases, news and features, to transmit the messages which will complement the marketing strategy. In this context there will be the task of preparing a matrix to ensure that all the positive points about the new product are transmitted. These will range from research findings on need for the product or its value, to information about the innovations incorporated, to statements from key figures in the company as to why the product is to be launched and the need it is to fulfil. The messages will be conveyed by the written and spoken word, photographs, graphs, support research, etc., and may include some of the marketing material developed to support the new product. In certain cases video and audio material will be prepared to support the presentation, which will be planned to introduce the new product to media and special interest groups. All facts used will need to be checked and double-checked, and any necessary authorization or legal clearances will need to be obtained.

- The matters of special event planning and direct mailings will be important ones in this PR context. They will include press briefings for specialist and general journalists and perhaps a special press launch, also special direct mailings to targeted groups. It is very likely that they will include other events which may be planned in relation to the marketing effort and where there could be a PR 'spin-off', for example a promotional tour.

- Finally there will be the important 'post-launch' phases of the operation, when the PR practitioner will be seeking to place material about the new product as a result of responses received (from the sales force, from media and from interested user groups). All this material must be collated and studied to provide a 'mirror' to the success of the launch operation so that there are additional publicity stories able to run and encourage further the marketing effort in support of the new product.

- In conclusion, the overall exercise must be evaluated against its predetermined plan, timing and budget, to establish the level of success achieved.

FOOTNOTE

Achieving perfect PR for a product clearly can be easier and more specific than obtaining the same result for a person, company or charity. Because, in marketing, the stakes can be high so resources can be easier to find and apply. But be careful, the integrity of the product itself must be such that the PR operation can succeed! Above all, avoid the temptation to try to present a sow's ear as if it were a silk purse!

8
PERFECT PR – FOR A CHARITY

Perfect PR for a charity is not easy. In fact it can be very difficult indeed. This is because many people think of charitable giving as their spontaneous and voluntary action – in making a donation, writing a cheque, or dropping a pound in the collecting box. They are right in part, but the whole matter of charitable giving or chequebook charity is only the tip of the iceberg. Charitable giving is more than good neighbourhood politics: today it represents – for a company – being a good corporate citizen. It is 'good' business as such. For charities, the whole area is in the process of being turned into 'big' business, needing a lot of commercial know-how, time, money and other resources devoted to it. Whether you are working in business, with responsibility for PR, or in the community, with a voluntary organization or charity, this is an area well worth detailed study.

Having said that, there are in this country hundreds and indeed thousands of charities – small, medium and large. Their praises are largely unsung, and most of them have to manage on pathetically slender resources. Yet, if the charities and the voluntary movement, two of the UK's strengths in terms of its social structure, were to disappear, no government – of any political climate – could afford to replace what they contribute, for nothing, to the social fabric of this nation.

But, as has been said earlier in this book, if the organization is not visible, to most people it does not exist. And, alas, most of the small and worthy charitable organizations in the UK are invisible, and so their voices are not heard and many people who would support their causes if they were familiar with them, do not do so.

PUTTING THE CASE, ACHIEVING VISIBILITY

So, how do you set about doing the perfect PR job for a charity?

The first move is to ensure that you have brought together all the information possible about your charity. When and how did it start? Why? What gap in the charitable world does it fill? Who relates to it? Where at the moment does it get its support from? Is it aided, in terms of a government grant? In terms of support from major (or minor) charitable trusts? From subscriptions from members? By earning money from special events? By contributions from industry or the public at large? Through the wills of former donors? How does it operate? Has it got sufficient resources? What programmes of work does it undertake? How successful is it in terms of securing support for its campaign? Has it a high public profile? Any public profile? How does it report on its campaigns and other activities? Has it any 'grass roots' membership? Any corporate membership? Is support growing or falling? Why? All these are questions which must be answered – and there will be many more, specialist to the area in which the charity operates.

The next move should be to examine which other charities or 'good causes' are near enough in their objectives to cause competition for the support of donors or possible sponsors or other corporate 'givers'. Is their support growing or falling? Why? Although often difficult, could co-operation be possible?

Now comes the task of making the charity's case. This entails putting on paper why the charity deserves support, where this could come from, and how it should be accessed. This will follow the traditional PR route of identifying and setting objectives, identifying target groups, agreeing messages to be transmitted and planning how to deliver them, against an agreed time frame

PERFECT PR

and budget. In turn, this will involve looking at the calendar of events and examining whether any of these are potentially of high enough profile to warrant national or regional or other specialist media support. If not, at least one event may have to be created to fill the gap.

All current items of print produced and distributed by the charity will need to be examined, also the current logo and house-style. Does this need to be updated or redesigned so that the charity's messages can be transmitted with more impact? This matter will need consideration and decision.

Now the PR practitioner involved in trying to help a charity will need to examine just what the charitable-giving marketplace is, and how to access this. Here is a snapshot which should be helpful in this context.

Corporate responsibility

Corporate responsibility or community sponsorship is now a powerful and growing medium in its own right. It can be used by charities to access funds. The majority of *The Times*' Top 100 companies in the UK are currently involved in community and/or charitable projects, and the level of their involvement is growing. Many multinational companies have foundations and trusts created for the specific purpose of charitable giving, so that they can gain tax advantage and focus their activity in this area. Indeed the more professional a company is in handling such activity the more the company and the community benefit as a result of its involvement.

Charitable giving

Charitable giving can really be divided into three parts:

1. *Individual giving.* This has been mentioned earlier; it relates to the individual's gift in cash or by cheque, or

even services or goods useful to the charity (e.g. food for a nursing home or a fund-raising event). In the US the whole subject of individual gifts of charity has been much further developed than in the UK. The Americans have made the process simpler – they have organized it, encouraged it, packaged and promoted it. It is run by professionals. In the UK we are still amateur in this area, but things are changing. Initiatives such as Comic Relief, Telethons and Children in Need have grown in popularity and provide a much-needed access to charitable funding for smaller charities needing additional resources.

2. *Corporate giving.* Sponsorship for the arts and other good causes has been actively promoted by the Government over recent years, whilst the creation of organizations such as The Prince's Trust and Business in the Community have given much needed injections of cash and other support from industry, whereby committed companies fund inner-city regeneration, training and environmental improvement. Creative links between industry and the community are without doubt beneficial to both sides, and extremely cost-effective in the long term. This could be a fruitful area for the PR practitioner to develop in relation to getting help for the charity in question. There are organizations which have been set up to help companies with their corporate giving, one of the best known of which is the Per Cent Club.

3. *Business partnerships.* The private sector has also taken steps, over recent years, to create, initiate and stimulate change by creating business–community partnerships. This has helped to establish roles as social service brokers, planners and builders of the social fabric of the country.

In turn, these developments are leading to companies

PERFECT PR

entering partnerships with public and non-profit making organizations to create better solutions to community problems, and this is good for everyone concerned.

THE MESSAGE TO INDUSTRY FROM A CHARITY

If you are the person involved in helping a worthy and charitable cause, you should recognize that the message to be delivered to the commercial organizations you have targeted needs to be focused, so that they can see it fits in with their own objectives. You will also need to incorporate the following messages so that they can be immediately accepted:

- When spending to support this charity you are spending wisely and productively because . . . [the reason needs to be spelt out, making the important points that the charity is of value to individuals, society at large, and also the organization specifically].
- Even one charitable event a year helps our cause, the community, and also your organization because . . . [again, spell out the reason].
- You can help us by giving in kind . . . [spell out what the charity needs: it could be access to experience (with someone joining a committee), it could be a second-hand PC or photocopier, it could be access to free photostatting, or sponsorship of a particular event].
- We will help you to involve management and staff in the community, by . . . [again, spell it out].
- Remember, involvement with our charity will help you to build a better business, and we will identify any help you give us by . . . [again, spell out if this will take the form of a list of supporters, a credit on the programme of an event, etc.].

EVALUATION

As with a company or a product, the means of evaluating the success of the charity's PR campaigns needs to be agreed in advance, so that the necessary and essential evaluation process can be carried out.

FOOTNOTE

If you are involved in PR activities for a charity, keep in mind at all times the basic ways in which charities help society. Charities help:

- to improve education
- to improve health
- to reduce poverty
- to support religions

Ensure that, in all your activities, you are identifying the areas in which your charity helps to improve the position for society at large.

9
BRUSHING UP ON YOUR PR SKILLS

So, you have decided to look more deeply into the area of PR, and you need to brush up your skills. This may be true whether you seek a career in PR, are already in PR, or if you have PR responsibilities within your company.

In this context you have to recognize the differences between *doing* PR, and being someone responsible for *using others to do* the PR to your specification.

How do you set about it?

The first step is to decide where your priorities lie.

DEVELOPING YOUR OWN INDIVIDUAL PR SKILLS
This means taking a hard look at your levels of current competence in relation to the traditional PR skills. These have been identified in an earlier chapter of this book.

Having identified which skills (or group of skills) you need to develop, there are many avenues available for you to explore in your search to improve your competence. For example:

- You may need to identify an essential reading list, with books and perhaps selected periodicals, to add to your existing knowledge in certain areas, and update it.
- You may need to access case history material, so that you can read how successful case histories, which may be relevant to your situation, were developed and implemented.
- You may need to study relevant research material.

- You may need to talk to experienced practitioners and see if you can identify someone who could act as an informal 'mentor' to you.
- You may decide to join one or more of the professional or trade associations in your specific area.
- You may need to enlist on selected study courses.
- You may decide that you need a particular professional qualification.
- You may decide you should do something to improve a first impression made on a stranger. First impressions are very important in PR terms. The matter of dress, speech etc. is critical. In the context of a job interview they could make all the difference in the world!

DEVELOPING YOUR PERFORMANCE AS A PR PRACTITIONER

If you are already involved in public relations, working for a company or other type of organization, it is more than likely that you are a member of the Institute of Public Relations. If you are not you certainly should be. This is the professional institute dedicated to providing a structure for the practice of public relations, as well as enhancing the ability and status of members. It operates a range of services of professional and personal benefit to members, and currently has a membership of nearly 5,000.

If you are working in a public relations consultancy, dealing with a number of clients' campaigns and needs in terms of professional PR, it is likely that you will have access to training opportunities. It is also relevant for you to be a member of the IPR in this case.

If you have the responsibility for PR operations within your company or organization

In this case your requirements may be somewhat different. However, it will be no bad thing if you brush up on your own PR skills and take the time and trouble to read about the subject, and find out as much as you can about how the different disciplines within it work.

Here again, there are many organizations which you could join and which could help you in this context. A relevant organization could be the Society of Consumer Affairs Professionals in Business, the UK arm of a US organization which represents those with responsibility for complaints handling and related functions in a company. SOCAP members are really the consumer's advocates in their organizations. Their address and telephone number is given on page 67.

Choosing which of the PR umbrella organizations is the right one for you to join is a matter to which you should give serious attention. Do, however, keep well in mind that joining an organization and paying your subscription is only dealing with the tip of the iceberg. What is even more important is to make your voice heard within the organization and to give it the time and attention to make the relationship profitable for you, your own company and the professional or business organization(s) you have joined. You want to feel, at the end of the day, that there is a dialogue of equals between you.

Continuing professional development

What you also need to recognize is that, today, training and competence should be ongoing. Indeed most professions are now requiring 'continuing professional development' of their memberships. This, in turn, relates to commitment of time, usually in three areas: Unstructured Learning, which includes time spent keeping up to date on developments in the profession or industry concerned, through reading the relevant periodicals and attending the key conferences and other events; Structured Learning, which includes time spent on courses where specific amounts of skills and/or knowledge are transferred; and time spent on achievement of specific and desirable professional qualifications.

And, even after the desirable benchmark qualifications are achieved, there is no letting up in the requirement to continue to learn. This is essential in an increasingly fast-moving and technological world. Since the area of public relations is so identified with the frontiers of development and change, you, the astute reader will recognize immediately the need to make a firm commitment to brushing up PR skills, both in your own interest and, even more importantly, in the interests of the organizations you work for and the consumers they serve.

On page 66 of this book there is a comprehensive section on Sources of Help to signpost you to the right organizations, books and other sources to access the type of help you may have decided you need.

10
THUMBNAIL CASE HISTORIES

WHEN A WHISPER IS WORTH MORE THAN A SHOUT

Challenge
A leading breakfast cereal manufacturer wished quietly to explore externally the benefits of addressing a change in diet, internally thought to improve consumer health – with resulting marketing potential.

PR solution
To call a medical symposium to discuss the differences between diseases in developed and developing countries. This was attended by key opinion formers interested in the relationship between diet and disease, with specific reference to the implications of fibre in the diet.

As the results are now there for all to see!

BREAKING A LOG-JAM IN DISTRIBUTION

Challenge
To establish a distribution channel for toiletries in supermarkets before the retail chains had recognized the advantages of broadening their sales base.

PR solution
Offering to handle an event for wives at the leading industry conference. Using the opportunity to present a most glamorous fashion show, linking diamonds and furs with very well-known compères and models, and with the most fabulous gems on show. With excellent hospitality, celebrity guests and a glittering occasion as a back drop, the chairman of the toiletries company

THUMBNAIL CASE HISTORIES

hosting the event was able to offer the ladies the chance to try the products by taking samples home with them.

The results of this pioneering exercise can be seen in the large displays given to toiletries in supermarkets throughout the country today!

USING A TELEPHONE LINK TO AID SECURITY

Challenge
A major shopping area was experiencing problems with regard to shoplifting, petty crime, etc. There was a major need for unobstrusive security links to be created and/or strengthened.

PR solution
To create a telephone link-up system between members of the trade body. This in turn was linked to the local police station. If there was a break in the link the police would know within minutes (because of the break in the receipt of phone calls) and, more importantly, just where the problem lay. This meant that they could move in to clear up the problem with minimum delay.

It worked; simply, practically – and cheaply too!

CREATING – AND DELIVERING – AN INTERNATIONAL MESSAGE

Challenge
To focus international attention on the plight of Berlin during the earliest and worst days of the Berlin Wall crisis – the 50s.

PR solution
To call a 'Berlin Festival of Fashion' during the opening weeks of a major new Berlin hotel – one of an international chain. Invited to the festival were leading

fashion journalists from the US and Europe. They all came. During the visit trips to the Brandenberg Gate and other focal points in Berlin were arranged.

The results could be seen in international stories carried in the media about the plight of 'brave little Berlin'. These, in turn, led to papers assigning 'Berlin Correspondents', so that Berlin's story was carried in newspapers throughout the world on all suitable occasions.

DEMONSTRATING LEADERSHIP

Challenge
To demonstrate a company's leadership of its market sector, without breaking the bank in terms of advertising spend!

PR solution
To pick a key issue – in this case the importance of Craft, Design and Technology, at the time a second-class subject in terms of the educational system – and to plan an intellectual project to demonstrate its importance to the future of the nation, and the desirability of giving the subject first-class status on the educational curriculum. As a result a series of educational lectures was planned over an entire decade. These took place in a prestigious venue with lecturers of first-class status and Chairmen of distinction. Invited audiences were a distillation of the leaders of the educational profession and industry. There were 'waiting lists' for all events, and the lectures were all published and distributed on request to many thousands of enquirers. A compilation of the lecture texts for the whole series was published and distributed at the end of the decade.

The results were substantial acknowledgements of the importance of the ethical contribution made by the sponsoring company, at a time when support for education was thin to say the least. In addition, schools were enthusiastic in their support for the educational programme of support, which the company had operated throughout the country for many years. *And* Design Technology was then firmly established on the Core Curriculum in education.

HELPING A NATION'S EXPORT EFFORT – AND, IN SO DOING, ENSURING THAT THE IMPORTING COUNTRY WAS NOT AT RISK

Challenge

To encourage agents of a major country's manufacturers to export to the UK as the result of a Trade Centre (a shop window for varying exhibits, to which interested trade buyers and relevant media are invited so that they can inspect the goods and services on offer). The particular problem was to ensure that the 'agents' representing each organization were 'responsible citizens' – in a situation where the country's laws meant that the facility was open to one and all, and it was not possible to 'ban' an undesirable agent. As a result there were real dangers that people who were not even able to hold bank accounts in the exporting country could be let loose, selling to prestigious UK retailers, with resultant and likely problems of lack of delivery of goods, loss of money, etc.

PR solution

To commission a leading journalist in each area, and to arrange a facility trip so that he or she could review the interested companies' merchandise, services and agents. Before the trip, efforts were made in the UK to research the companies concerned, and the potential agents they were due to appoint the task of selling to the UK. As a result, each journalist was fully briefed and could 'discourage' those who were felt to be undesirable or unsuitable for the purpose.

Over several years the formulas developed on behalf of

this operation were so successful they were copied by several other countries – including the UK!

DEFUSING AN INDUSTRIAL DISPUTE

Challenge
To help defuse a major industrial dispute in a company whose employees were very sports-minded.

PR solution
Since the workforce was very sports-minded, it was natural that the company was involved in sports sponsorship in a big way. At the time there was a sports personality who was extremely well known, very warm and very popular. A visit to a major plant was arranged for this personality, and the occasion gave the opportunity for both sides of the dispute to contribute together to make the event a success – in spite of the problems both sides were involved in. This, in turn, helped to break the 'log-jam', and in due course solutions were found to the dispute so that both sides could accept a compromise. New personal connections had been made, and each side found that using them was advantageous.

SEEING BOTH SIDES – WITH HUMOUR

Challenge
A major organization was holding its first conference. One of the key areas to be discussed was industrial relations. The Director General wanted a woman speaker (rare in those days) to make a point she felt was important, with humour.

PR solution
To make as glamorous an appearance as possible (in a formal pink trouser suit!) and to speak on industrial relations in terms of the marriage bed. The key point

made was that, in the case of a tense, traumatic marriage breakdown, there is little if any chance of both parties sharing the same bedroom and bed for the future! In the case of industrial disputes there will be a time when both sides have to work together again, and so the prime objective must be to avoid the total breakdown of communications between the parties involved on a personal basis.

The results were good – the point was made with lightness and some humour and the audience reacted by laughing and clapping – and there were many comments that the speaker had been recognized as not 'union bashing'!

GETTING STARTED

Challenge
To inaugurate a national initiative on money education.

PR solution
Remember two facts: (i) Most people prefer to say 'yes' than 'no' in most circumstances, and (ii) If you ask people to give a defined, modest amount of time to explore an important idea, they are likely to agree. Three short meetings of a small group (representing the financial services industry, the consumer and education) were held to explore whether or not there was room for an initiative to help people to understand their personal finances. The conclusion was that such an initiative could be very well worthwhile. As a result a new national charity was founded which, whilst modest in terms of finance, has a worthy track-record, now acknowledged in government and regulatory circles as well as by relevant education, consumer and industry bodies. It is doing much good work and its activities have been covered by the national media on many occasions.

11
SOURCES OF HELP AND INFORMATION

In a brief book of this nature, 'signposting' to indicate sources of help and information takes a high priority. There is much which needs to be learnt and absorbed about how to achieve effective and successful standards of performance in public relations. The author is indebted to the Public Relations Consultants Association, the lead body for the consultancies operating in the whole area of public relations activity, for much of the information contained in this section.

USEFUL BOOKS

The Principles of Public Relations by Harold Oxley (Kogan Page)

Professional Communications for a Change by Hans Johnsson (Prentice Hall)

Getting the Message Across by Marie Jennings and David Churchill (Simon & Schuster for The Institute of Directors)

Public Relations in Practice – a Casebook edited by Danny Moss (Routledge)

USEFUL PERIODICALS

PR Week
Marketing
Marketing Week
Campaign
The Economist
The Director
Management Today

SOURCES OF CASE HISTORY MATERIAL

The Public Relations Consultants Association
The Institute of Public Relations

SOURCES OF HELP AND INFORMATION

SOURCES OF RESEARCH MATERIAL
City of London Business School
The Public Relations Consultants Association

KEY ORGANIZATIONS

The Institute of Public Relations, The Old Trading House, 15 Northburgh Street, London EC1V 0PR (Telephone 0171-253 5151)

The Public Relations Consultants Association, Willow House, Willow Place, London SW1P 1JH (Telephone 0171-233 6026)

CAM (Communication, Advertising and Marketing Education Foundation – the examinations board for public relations, advertising and marketing), Abford House, 15 Wilton Road, London SW1V 1NJ (Telephone 0171-828 7506)

SOCAP (Society of Consumer Affairs Professionals in Business – United Kingdom), 150 Church Hill Road, Cheam, Sutton, Surrey SM3 8NF (Telephone 0181-715 7705)

PROFESSIONAL QUALIFICATIONS

Today there are many professional qualifications in public relations on offer. These include:

CAM Diploma in Public Relations, Dip (PR)CAM

Watford/PRCA Diploma in International Public Relations, West Herts College

MSc in Public Relations, The University of Stirling

CNAA BA (Hons) in Public Relations, Bournemouth University

Diploma in Public Relations, Dublin Institute of Technology, College of Commerce (Dublin)

CNAA BA in Communication, Napier University (Edinburgh)

BA (Hons) in Public Relations, College of St Mark and St John (Plymouth)

MA in Public Relations, Manchester Metropolitan University

PR JARGON

In the world of PR, as in other specialist business areas, there is an overwhelming urge to use the jargon of the business. This is often quite simply inexplicable to others. Here is a note of some of the most often used jargon with a line of explanation.

Account Executive – sometimes called *Account Handler*, or *Consultant* – The executive appointed by a public relations consultancy to liaise with a particular client of the consultancy.

Advertorial – The use of paid-for advertising space to present information in an editorial format.

Billing – The assessment of the revenue from fees and expenditures enjoyed by a public relations consultancy.

Briefing – The assessment or informal presentation of fact, opinion or background information given at meetings to media or selected groups of people.

Brand Manager – The executive in a company with responsibility for the marketing activities of a major 'branded' product produced by that company.

Copy – Words in a press release, advertisement, poster or other visual or audio script.

Focus Group – The carefully selected small group of people who have a shared interest in hearing what an organization has to say about a particular situation.

Image – The known 'profile' of a person or an organization – the perception of them.

Lobbying – The campaign name for a series of meetings

to brief particularly selected persons or organizations about a specific issue, programme or campaign with a view to gaining their support for it. Most often used in connection with Parliamentary Lobbying.

Opinion Former – A person identified as important to the company in terms of being in a position to influence others, on a national or specialist basis.

Pitch – A presentation, with supporting documentation, whereby a company or a person seeks appointment to responsibilities for developing and delivering a PR programme or campaign, either internally (as a person with PR responsibilities) or from the outside (by a public relations consultancy).

Presenter – The person charged with presenting a television programme or, alternatively, fronting a series of meetings.

Public Relations/Public Affairs/Communications/Corporate Communications – These phrases are often mixed up and used as the spirit moves the person or the company concerned. Most often used to designate a job function or responsibility. If there are differences they are the following:

- *Public Relations* – General, and can cover everything within internal and external communications responsibilities.
- *Public Affairs* – Most often related to the corporate affairs of a company and its relations with its prime target groups, such as shareholders, and opinion formers, such as legislators.
- *Communications* – Again loosely used, more specifically relates to planning, organizing and implementing the use of communications 'tools' – for example publicity, print, events, etc.

- *Corporate Communications* – Includes all the above and relationships between the organization and its key stakeholders (from shareholders to the community in general, as well as opinion formers).

(Today, it is likely that the Director of Public Affairs or Corporate Communications will be just one step away from the main board of a company, and already there are a few who are members of the boards of their organizations.)

Story Board – The rough visual treatment to be used for a television programme, advertisement or similar film material.

Visual – The rough sketch of illustrations proposed in a leaflet, advertisement, or similar document.

It goes without saying that the list of additional PR jargon phrases can be a long one!